SOMETHING
Beautiful

Why Settle When Life Can Be Beautiful?

Jackie Tinkler   Amber Edwards

WESTBOW
P R E S S®
A DIVISION OF THOMAS NELSON
& ZONDERVAN

WestBow Press books may be ordered through booksellers or by contacting:

WestBow Press
A Division of Thomas Nelson & Zondervan
1663 Liberty Drive
Bloomington, IN 47403
www.westbowpress.com
1 (866) 928-1240

Headshot Image Credits:

Heather D. Whidden, Photographer and Owner
"Reflections of" Photography for Amber Edwards
Nadia Wilder Photography for Jackie Tinkler

ISBN: 978-1-9736-7863-2 (sc)
ISBN: 978-1-9736-7865-6 (hc)
ISBN: 978-1-9736-7864-9 (e)

Library of Congress Control Number: 2019917593

Print information available on the last page.

WestBow Press rev. date: 01/06/2020

Contents

Acknowledgments

We would like to thank, first and foremost, our Lord and Savior, Jesus Christ, for it is only through him that we are overcomers. Because of his constant work in our lives, we are both in a place where we can share our life stories with others.

We would also like to thank all the amazing people the Lord has placed in our lives throughout this journey. There have been so many precious friends, way too many to list or even count, who have lifted us up in prayer, stood with us, fought for our breakthroughs, mentored us, offered sound advice, supported our dreams, and spoken words of encouragement; most importantly, they have loved us through this journey and throughout our lives.

Thank you to our church family and the leadership teams at the Grants Mill and Greystone campuses of Church of the Highlands in Birmingham, Alabama, especially Pastor Charles Kelley, for speaking life into us and encouraging us throughout this journey. To our senior pastor, Chris Hodges, whose wisdom and love of God's Word, which he shares with such ease of understanding, has helped us grow in our walks and encouraged us to keep taking our next step.

Special Thanks from Jackie

Thank you to my husband, Jim, and daughter, Lauren, for traveling this long road with me, listening to my crazy dreams and schemes, supporting and loving me always. I love you to the moon. Special thanks to my parents, Bill and Donna, for nurturing the love for God, friends, and family and also for all the fun. To my Lulu for being the best grandmother, who listened to my stories and served me coffee and Italian toast at her kitchen table every Saturday morning. And to Aunt Maryann for being a great spiritual mentor.

Special Thanks from Amber

Thank you to my mother, who instilled strong moral values in me and made sure I was raised in church and knew the truth of God's Word. To my Mamaw, who was one of the most loving and godly women I will ever know this side of heaven. Mamaw, so much of who I am today is because of you. To my precious husband, Michael, for always, always, always believing in me and being my biggest cheerleader. Your love and support are what keep me going, even on the toughest of days. On the days when I'm just sad, you're my happy. To my daughter Shelby, who made me a mom and truly is my "mini me": I love hanging out with you and am so thankful that the Lord gave me a daughter and lifelong bestie, all rolled into one amazing gift from above. To my son Zac, you were (and are) God's answer to my prayer that I would have an amazing little boy to love. Each and every day, I am proud of the man of character you are becoming, and I can't wait to see all that the Lord has in store for you.

Michael, Shelby, and Zac, thank you all for putting up with me and for being so understanding when I've had to sacrifice time away from home to build my ministry and write my story so that others may see that there can be an abundant life, even after hurt. You three make my life truly beautiful, and I love you with my whole heart for my whole life.

Just a Note

Friends, we are so thrilled you have decided to join us on our *Something Beautiful* journey, where we will discover that we don't have to settle. To the contrary, as we grow in relationship and know God more and more, we can begin to enjoy the beautiful life he has waiting for us.

We wrote this book because so much of each of our life's journey has been similar, yet the distinct stories and giftings each of us have blend to make the study complete. There are many personal stories, unique to our specific journey, woven throughout these pages. You will note we have placed our name at the top of these stories, so you will have a point of reference and begin to feel as if you are getting to know us, and we can't wait to get to know you too.

So whether you are meeting in a cozy home setting, at a local coffee shop, or in another location, we want you to know we're cheering you on as if we're right there with you. Amber will need a big ol' glass of unsweet tea (with lots of ice), and as you arrive, she will give you her most encouraging "Hey, sister!"

Meanwhile, go ahead and get Jackie's hot cup of coffee ready (decaf, please) and expect a big hug and a "Hey girl". We want you to come on in, relax, and get comfortable, whether that's holding a glass of tea, sipping on a cup of coffee, kicking off your shoes, or putting your hair up. Take a deep breath, and release whatever the day left sitting in your lap or weighing on your mind; this is time for you. So get ready to share some sister time as we grow and learn together through love, laughter, and loads of encouraging scripture from God's Word.

We can't wait to dive into the study with you, share a few laughs, meditate on God's Word, and find something beautiful along the way.

Enjoy the study.

Introduction

He has made everything beautiful in its time. He
has also set eternity in the hearts of men; yet they
cannot fathom what God has done from beginning
to end. (Ecclesiastes 3:11 BSB)

Jackie's Story

One sunny day in Upstate New York, I strolled to the tiny grocery,
where I bought all the candy I could get into my pocket for five
dollars. This particular day was different from life today. It was the
1970s, and I could walk by myself and feel fairly safe. I didn't feel
completely secure again for a long while after that.

It seems like a lifetime ago, and carried a freedom only a child
could know, a place where a young mind is free from pressure, where
time is a friend with nowhere to go, a young heart free to create, live
in the moment, and be swept away with curiosity. There are no dumb
questions or wrong things to wear; just summer, all year around.

Those were carefree days, but a day would come when the
sunshine would fade and green leaves, turning brown, would fall to
the ground. It was the pathway to winter, where the cold makes its
roaring entrance and the sounds of summer are no more.

Somewhere between childhood and young adulthood, the joy of my beautiful day had ended. When I was a young woman, life and its circumstances would turn away from the sun, and a new wind would blow. The winds of change would gather my dreams into its gust and try to destroy the beauty of summer as it whispered tales of woe into my ear. Words from long ago would become the theme inside my head: *You are ugly*. Believing this to be true, I would live in the background of insecurity, where fear imprisoned my mind. The only thing to do was hide in a world of pretend for comfort. My fantasies became my refuge and confidence, where I was a rock star, a model, and an actress. There I was beautiful, accepted, and self-assured, but in the real world, I was barely visible to anyone.

I knew God but didn't quite have the confidence to follow him. Part of me wanted the acceptance of the world, but another part of me knew I was different. Left to my own ways, I went in search of the world's love and acceptance but always ended up disappointed and on the wrong road. This was until I decided to walk a different path and make one decision that would change the course of my history for the better. I decided to be all in, and that is where I discovered real beauty and became more than I thought I was.

I would become the beauty of God's heart

One Decision

Some of us may have had a light connection with Jesus through our lives. We know him, but we don't serve him. Perhaps you were not raised to know him, or you were introduced to him and decided to follow your own way. For those of you who need a second chance or even if you have not had the privilege of being introduced, it starts with a simple recognition.

Let's pray: Lord Jesus, I recognize you are the Savior. Only you can forgive me from sin and cleanse me from living without you. I desire to go in a different direction and invite you into my life as Savior and Lord; fill my heart with love, and help me to live a changed life, restoring hope and my eternal salvation through the power of your resurrection and a personal relationship with you.

PART 1.

The Realization

"

Satan wants
us to believe that one mistake
can taint us for the rest of our lives,
but that's not what God's Word says

Chapter 1

I Had It All Wrong

We Are Not Stuck. We can wake up to the realization that maybe, just maybe, we don't have all the answers.

Amber's Story

Have you ever felt like a victim of your circumstances? Helpless to ever have a normal life because of something in your past? Perhaps you've convinced yourself that whatever may have happened to you is destined to write the chapters of your story still to come?

Satan will use whatever tiny seed of negativity he can to convince us we're victims: stained, tainted, and unable to ever be wanted, happy, successful, or, heaven forbid, used by God.

Many years ago, I had the privilege of teaching fifth and sixth grade girls Sunday school at my church. I absolutely adored each one of those precious girls. We had a good-sized group of regular attenders and were always doing something fun: pottery outings, spa nights, crafting afternoons, secret pal exchanges, and so on. Our class quickly became the one all the younger girls eagerly looked forward to entering.

Each week, I was challenged to make whatever portion of God's Word we were studying relevant and exciting, in the hope that each girl would grow in her faith and ultimately desire a deep and lasting relationship with the Lord. I used games, crafts, and illustrations to engage each of those preteens while weaving God's truth into their hearts.

I rejoiced as I witnessed the light-bulb moments when, finally, a portion of the Word that perhaps never made any sense before suddenly was as clear as freshly cleaned glass.

And then came the story of David and Bathsheba. Yikes.

Can we say not necessarily a kid-friendly kind of story? To be honest, it reads more like a Harlequin romance novel, yet there it is, right in the middle of the Old Testament. I remember thinking to myself, *Maybe we could skip this week and go off book*, but God prompted me to share the story just as written in his Word.

It was a challenging lesson, but we made it through. As we were wrapping up, allowing a few minutes for comment, I recall one of the girls nonchalantly saying, "She [Bathsheba] was a victim." We never discussed that thought; thank goodness, it was approaching time to go, so we closed in prayer and got the girls to big church on time.

If you're unfamiliar with the story of David and Bathsheba, it is the picture of lust and adultery from the very minute David lays his eyes on Bathsheba. He sees her bathing and immediately wants her for his own. So he inquires as to who this bathing beauty is; although he quickly learns she's a married woman, that doesn't stop him. He summons for Bathsheba to be brought to him and has his way with her.

In reading through the story again, well over a decade since teaching it to those precious preteens, I recalled the "victim" statement. What insight at such a young age.

The Word doesn't tell us whether Bathsheba consented to David's advances or not, although I have to believe she really didn't have much choice, as her husband was away and David *was* the king of Israel. But what was supposed to have been a one-night stand quickly turned into anything but when Bathsheba realizes she's pregnant. The story goes on to tell how David takes matters into his own hands, and adultery eventually turns into murder. Oh, what a tangled web of lies and heartbreaking circumstances Bathsheba found herself in. It would have been easy, even understood perhaps, for her to take on this victim mentality. She had, after all, betrayed her husband, which ultimately led to his murder by way of an unwanted pregnancy.

But Bathsheba did not fall into that trap. She trusted God and allowed him to work in her life. As her story concludes, we see that not only does God elevate her to a position of honor as Queen Mother over the nation of Israel, but the Savior of the world ultimately comes from her lineage.

Satan wants us to believe that one mistake can taint us for the rest of our lives, but that's *not* what God's Word says.

No matter the devastation of our past, we don't have to be victims of our circumstances. Even if we have it wrong today, God promises that our beautiful day is coming.

Father, we pray for our sisters in Christ to find your true beauty in their hearts. We pray the wounds of the past will be forgotten and cleansed by your abundant love. Give us joy where there had been ashes, and make the sun shine bright again where we can live fearlessly and be a light shining in the darkness.

Beautiful Moment

In your own words, define the word *beautiful*. Be as real as possible about what you feel true beauty is at this point in your life. Take into account what you have been told, what you have experienced, and what you really think or feel in your heart to be true about beauty.

_____

_____

_____

_____

_____

_____

_____

_____

_____

_____

Jackie's Story

Growing up in my teen and early adult years, what I thought was beautiful honestly completely escaped me. My sense of self-worth came from how I thought I looked on the outside. The world was my mirror, and it said I was not pretty enough, good enough, or confident enough. Most people thought I was shy or quiet, but the truth is, I was untrusting and insecure. I held my talents, personality, and gifts back for fear of rejection and cared way too much what people thought. Those early years became a wasteland of preoccupation and self-absorption. This fantasy life I had created overshadowed real life, and for a long time, it kept me from finding my true purpose. I was wrong.

The lies of the enemy may sound good at the time, but we sure do waste a lot of life believing them.

It's time to turn our thoughts around!

Being wrong doesn't mean you can't be right again. Tell God where you went wrong, and ask him to forgive you for going your own way. He will grant you understanding; he longs to give you a fresh start.

Prayer of Repentance: Father, I was wrong, and I'm sorry. From this day forward, I'm going to walk a different way. I'm turning my back on the wrong path, sin, and I'm going to change for the better.

> I know I distressed you greatly with my letter. Although I felt awful at the time, I don't feel at all bad now that I see how it turned out. The letter upset you, but only for a while. Now I'm glad—not that you were upset, but that you were jarred into turning things around. You let the distress bring you to God, not drive you from him. The result was all gain, no loss. (2 Corinthians 7:8–9 MSG)

Paul's words are a beautiful picture of celebration and gladness over a change of heart.

Let's Be Honest

What are some of the thoughts you believe about yourself? About God? About others?

_____

_____

_____

_____

_____

_____

_____

_____

_____

What do you tell yourself to bring comfort and make you feel better?

_____

_____

_____

_____

_____

_____

_____

_____

_____

_____

Where might you need a change of direction to follow God's best plan for your life?

_____

_____

_____

_____

_____

_____

_____

_____

_____

Beautiful Moment

† There are no worthless people.

† There is not a single life God can't redeem and give value to.

Remember, ladies:

> We are always learning and becoming a person of value … the person God already sees!

> Those who look to him are radiant; their faces are never covered with shame. (Psalm 34:5 NIV)

Those who look to God for their life are _____.

We often describe someone whose beauty catches our attention as "radiant," showing a beautiful light from within. This special glow doesn't come from a brand of cosmetic or its careful application. No, it's God himself living on the inside and truly radiating out.

For so long, the pursuit of being physically beautiful meant finding love, but I had it wrong. True beauty is a woman who has found her identity in Christ and has a personal relationship with him. Strength, dignity, and the confidence of knowing who we are in Christ is our beauty because it is the love and radiance of the Lord himself that makes us beautiful.

Jackie's Story

Being an old soul at heart, I love the golden era of classic movies. In my living room, I have a beautiful romantic book cabinet, circa 1900, that displays more than fifty (and counting) classic movies from the 1930s and 1940s. One of my favorites in the collection is a 1944 movie called *Mr. Skeffington,* starring Bette Davis (Fanny) and Claude Raines (Job). It is the classic story of beauty, love, rejection, and ultimately what truly matters. It's almost hard to watch, actually, but the message at the end is so poignant. Fanny, a once irresistible, self-consumed socialite and beauty, descends a magnificently appointed staircase toward her estranged husband, Job. He's come back blind and poor but has been the only one who has ever truly loved her. Fanny, now ravaged by an illness that has taken her once-captivating beauty, is now old and alone. As she nears the bottom of the staircase, Job senses her presence. He confesses the secret of love that Fanny now will learn, as her physical beauty has faded: "A woman is beautiful when she's loved, and only then." You see, *love* is what makes us beautiful.

Take a moment and read 1 Corinthians 13. According to this passage of scripture, write a list of what love is:

_____   _____

_____   _____

_____   _____

_____   _____

_____   _____

Write the list of what love is not:

_____   _____

_____   _____

_____   _____

_____   _____

Not knowing the love of Jesus hurts. Yikes, here is where it can lead us if we don't find it:

❖ We're self-consumed.

❖ We're looking for love in toxic relationships.

❖ Our priorities are out of order.

❖ We have no clear direction or path for our life.

❖ We have unbalanced eating and spending habits.

❖ We can become needy and dependent on others for what only God can give us.

Are any of these areas currently impacting your life, or have they done so in the past?

_____

_____

_____

_____

_____

_____

_____

Make a decision today to get healthy spiritually, emotionally, and physically. Jot down one step you can take starting today.

_____

_____

_____

Now, find a godly friend to keep
you on track. Ready, set, go.

You've got this, girl.

What matters is not your outer appearance—the
styling of your hair, the jewelry you wear, the cut of
your clothes—but your inner disposition. (1 Peter
3:3–4 MSG)

According to this scripture what does the hidden beauty of the
heart look like?

_____

_____

A gentle and quiet spirit is our best feature. This is not to say we
can't be assertive or enjoy dress up, makeup or looking well, however,
it's the inner character of our spirit, where beauty never fades, that
becomes the focus rather than the focal.

What three things does 1 Peter 3:3–5 tell us about the inner
beauty of a beautiful, confident woman?

It is the _____
of a _____
that is of _____.

Now attempt, at this early point in the study to rewrite the
definition of beauty.

_____

_____

_____

_____

_____

_____

Father, give my sisters rest and refreshment from their daily commitments. I pray all are exalted and honored for the beautiful women they are and for their faithfulness. Where they are weak, be their strength. If they feel less than or incapable in any way, where the enemy has come in like a flood, lift up a wall against him so no strategy or weapon will win. Let them know how beautiful they are to you and to others because your spirit resides inside them. Speak words of affirmation, edification, and kindness to them through others that will build them up. Sing over them while they sleep, and give them revelation and words of wisdom for each day. Let them know it's okay, and all is well. I ask this for my friends in the precious and comforting name of Jesus.

Deep Thoughts and Reflections

Before going any further in the study, spend some time thinking about how you truly feel God sees you or has seen you in the past.

Remember, this exercise is for you only; no one else will see it, so be very honest with yourself. Jot down your thoughts and feelings here. Please don't skip this exercise, as we will be looking back on it as we conclude the study.

_____

_____

_____

_____

_____

_____

_____

_____

_____

_____

_____

_____

WHAT TENDS
TO GET IN
THE WAY OF MY
BEAUTIFUL LIFE,
MY BEAUTIFUL DAY,
MY SOMETHING MORE
IS MY THINKING

Chapter 2

I Had to Let It Go

I Can Let It Go; I Can Forgive. What if I refocused
my life around Jesus so I could have a new life?

As women, most of us can say we have mastered putting on a brave
or pretty face when we need to do so. On the inside, we may be
frustrated, angry, or resentful that life hasn't gone the way we hoped.
Maybe there is an inner turmoil we can't quite put our finger on,
but we know something isn't quite right. Maybe that comment our
friend made the other day just didn't sit right with us, but we didn't
say anything. Or that post we saw on Facebook from our beautiful
friend, who appears to have everything, upset us but we posted a
"You go, girl" comment, when in all reality, we are feeling jealous
and envious. Maybe we overcommit and say yes to something we
don't want to do or can't do, and then we feel resentment the whole
time we are doing it. What about the woman whose life is falling
apart? No one seems to understand her daily stress. She is hurting
inside but continues to smile, all the while telling everyone around
her, "I'm fine," but secretly, she's angry that no one has seen her need.

We all have struggles and commitments we stress about, and it's
only a matter of time before someone doesn't meet our expectations.
It's at this point that we are faced with an opportunity to be better

or to be bitter. In these moments, there will be many who are more than glad to write our script for the day, but you and I have a choice in how we respond.

God's grace is the catalyst to overcoming not only our past hurts but also our daily offenses. When we are trapped in a cycle of rejection and unforgiveness, we have an acute awareness of pain and the need for help. Jesus has provided our way out of carrying hurt and offense. Because Jesus forgave me, I can then in turn forgive others. Out of the gratitude of my heart, I can understand that I am no better than any other human being on the face of the planet not to extend the hand of forgiveness. It's not a feeling, but a choice, so that I can be in a place of freedom with God and others. I am essentially giving that person to God, all of their ugliness and the pain they caused me, and asking God to now deal with them. I don't have to exact any revenge or hatred. On the contrary, the way of forgiveness is surrendering it to God and letting it go.

Think of a current hurt or offense you've allowed yourself to stew over or sit in for a while. Ask the Lord to forgive you, commit to forgiving whoever wronged you, and decide to let it go. Now, say this out loud with me: "Let it go!"

Beautiful Moment

Forgiveness is not a feeling but a choice,
so that I can be in a place of freedom with God and others.

There are times when we can't really point to a reason, but something just isn't right. We're just unhappy, depressed, or perhaps even angry, and we honestly don't know why. These moments are hard to identify, and it feels like even my fellowship with God is stale. I don't quite hear him the way I used to, and I can feel my heart becoming hard and calloused. In these moments, it's time to check yourself. Maybe you're harboring a little bit of unchecked anger. It may be we have held onto an offense and are finding it hard to forgive. It may also be all our unchecked anger and unforgiveness has developed into a bitter attitude. One sure way to know is when we've been offended, we just can't seem to stop talking negatively about the offender. Her name comes up in conversation, and we're all too ready to tell everyone *exactly* what she did. No, girlfriend. Do you really want to go through life without a smile? Of course you don't, so forgive.

> See to it that no one fails to obtain the grace of God and that no bitter root grows up and causes you trouble, or many of you will become defiled. (Hebrews 12:15 ISV)

Girl, bitter is not beautiful.

Bitterness … oh, what a loaded word. When I hear it, no matter the context, it gives me a twinge of anxiety and causes my mind to wander to different crevices of my heart. Some of these filled long ago, but others are still very tender, even today. It's in those tender places that I can feel the sting start to move straight up from my heart to my mind in an attempt to take my thoughts captive. The feeling of bitterness certainly isn't exclusive to me, to us as women, or even to our generation.

In the book of 1 Samuel, as we read the story of Michal, we see this dangerous feeling was "large and in charge" right in the tangled web of her life. When we meet Michal, we quickly learn that she's a princess. I'm not talking about a princess like you and I may joke about being or that our moms may warn our soon-to-be spouses we *think* we are. No, she was actually a true princess, the daughter of King Saul.

She found herself enamored with David, who her father was not so fond of. There were clearly some jealously issues there, since David had been handpicked by God to be the future king. Here the story begins to read like another Harlequin novel as Saul, with a sinister ulterior motive, gives his daughter to David to be his wife, while quickly setting into motion plans to kill his new son-in-law. Michal loves David so she betrays her father; she helps David escape, and he goes into hiding. While David is on the run for years, both he and Michal marry again. Saul dies. David becomes king, demands the return of his wife, Michal, and steals her away from her new husband; goodness, all this happened in Biblical times?

Although Michal is now a queen, life certainly isn't perfect. The Word says Michal develops a heart of bitterness against David, and the story sadly concludes with a lonely and childless Michal, who appears to live out her days separated from David. Depressing, right?

Though the Word doesn't go into detail about why Michal ended up such a bitter soul, I can only imagine there were many *should have, could have,* and *what if* thoughts she probably wrestled with. Not unlike Michal and maybe yourself, these questions sometimes keep me up at night. When I begin to question how my life has played out, it's easy to feel that splinter of bitterness begin to grow into a branch or, heaven forbid, I let it become a full-size tree. You see, the shade of that bitterness tree can begin to cover us, and it's easy to find ourselves resting there. In those moments, the enemy wants us to be angry and let the hurt take over. He will lie to us and make us believe that we have to live there in our bitterness.

> Each heart knows its own bitterness, and no one else can share its joy. (Proverbs 14:10 NIV)

Which splinters are keeping your wounds of bitterness open? The betrayal of a spouse, ex-husband, or boyfriend? Feelings of abandonment by a parent? Perhaps in-laws who seem to completely discount your feelings or those of your children? A boss you feel doesn't value you or completely overlooks your hard work? Maybe a friend who walked away at a time you really needed her? Choose today to confront the un-pulled roots of bitterness you may have left growing and yank them right on out of your life, so you can experience true joy and happiness and not look back with any regrets.

Recently, a beautiful friend of mine unknowingly threw me under the bus in conversation with a mutual friend. As it was happening, I was completely stunned. I could not believe these specific words were coming from her lips. I immediately felt the need to defend myself, to make it right, or to just run away. It was so wrong. I knew my friend did not intentionally mean to betray me in that way, but it was so hard to not want to stay angry. As she was talking, she didn't even miss a beat, not realizing what she was doing.

Well, anyway, I might have fumed and been hurt for a day or two, but I realized I had to make it right and reconcile the anger in my heart toward her. The me of my past would have closed up and ran, but that's not who I am anymore. I have a new heart, and I can deal with this.

First, I told myself the truth:

† There is no need to fear; God will defend you.

† This is a misunderstanding.

† My friendship means more to me, so I will try to understand from God's point of view.

Second, I decided

† I will go to my friend in a loving, gentle way,

† I will clear up any misunderstanding,

† I will forgive my friend from my heart, and

† I will let it go.

As it turned out, once I forgave and decided to let it go, I realized my friend never intended to hurt me. The Lord revealed to me that this was an area of growth in her that he was already working on.

You see, it doesn't matter how amazing our lives are, how much money we have, what position we hold in the community, or even if we're royalty. When we allow ourselves to believe the lies of the enemy and harbor hurt or bitterness in our hearts, we will never be at peace and things others do *to* us will always be our focus, instead of what God is doing *in* us.

May we never forget that, like Michal, we are princesses, true daughters of the King of Kings. Let's not allow ourselves to be destroyed by harboring destructive feelings.

> Create in me a clean heart, O God, and renew a
> right spirit within me. (Psalm 51:10 BSB)

Some of us will go through things that are not so easily mended. Even if the relationship is broken, we can still forgive; however, it often takes time to build trust and go all in again. We must release them with a loving heart and attitude, and let God bring about the changes and soften the heart. This is challenging, but you can do it.

I can do all things through Christ who strengthens me. (Philippians 4:13 NKJV)

Forgiveness Prayer

Father, I release _____ [offender's name] to you in the name of Jesus. I forgive _____ for _____.
Father, help me to now walk in forgiveness. I won't continue to tell the story, slander, or shame the person who offended me. I ask you to wash me clean of anything I have done to contribute to any hatred, bitterness, or ill feelings. I am sorry for harboring unforgiveness in my heart, and I fully release _____ to your love.

The only way to walk in the sun again is to let go of anyone and everyone who has hurt or offended us. This is now God's business, and you need to be free to live a life of love and joy, walking a new path of wholeness of being forgiven and extending forgiveness.

Beautiful Moment

Girls, take a moment to read each of the following scriptures aloud and answer the questions. Be prepared to discuss with the group and commit to pray for one another. You and God have this.

> Be tolerant of one another and forgive each other if anyone has a complaint against another. Just as the Lord has forgiven you, you also should forgive. (Colossians 3:13 ISV)

According to the above scripture, why should we forgive?

> Be angry, yet do not sin. Do not let the sun set while you are still angry, and do not give the Devil an opportunity to work. (Ephesians 4:26–27 ISV)

According to Ephesians 4 above, what will happen if we don't take care of an offense quickly?

_____

_____

> Don't take revenge, dear friends. Instead, let God's anger take care of it. After all, Scripture says, "I alone have the right to take revenge. I will pay back," says the Lord. (Romans 12:19 GW)

Tell about a time you may have taken matters in your own hands. What was the outcome?

_____

_____

_____

_____

_____

_____

_____

_____

Let it go.
Everything doesn't have
to be perfect.

Jackie's Story

As I'm looking out the window of a beautifully decorated cabin in Mentone, Alabama, I see trees for miles. Some are a dingy brown, and others have white patches of moss and fungus. There are a few whose buds are trying to spring up, and I am sure they will be beautiful in just a few short weeks. The sky is gray, and it looks like rain. Not the picture-perfect weather I intended for a writing weekend. I told Amber on the way over, I felt like everything had to be perfect before I could embark on this wonderfully creative weekend. I'll need to have a pedicure, my hair should be washed, I'll be wearing something trendy but comfortable. I can't forget my favorite candle and blanket. And the weather; the weather should be great. There go those high expectations again, like I'm waiting for some big burst of rightness to happen.

We all know life does not work like this. If you have been on this merry-go-round for any length of time, girlfriend, we're just going to have to find some perspective and enjoy the ride. What tends to get in the way of my beautiful life, my beautiful day, my something more, is my thinking. To find my happy place, I have to get my thoughts fixed in the right direction. We should be on the yellow brick road, heading toward the truth that saves our day, right? The only way this happens for me is if I move myself out of the way and trust God to lead me down my happy path, even in the midst of uncertainty, daily annoyances, and bad days. We can find our happy place, serve God, and overcome the bad days by changing our thinking and practicing a little patience. Allow God's grace and peace to work within, then a new perspective and the strength and hope to walk through anything will lead you to the place you want to be.

Beautiful Moment

The Lord says "I will guide you along the BEST pathway for your life, I will advise you and watch over you." (Psalm 32:8 NLT)

God's pathway is _____ for me.
He _____ me, _____ me,
and _____ over me.

The word of God
changes our hearts,
and shapes our
"happy"!

Let go and trust as he leads us to our best outcome. We may be tempted to leave God's path when we don't see where it's going. On one of my most frustrating days, I've heard myself say, "I can fix this so much faster." Yes, I said that. My temporary fix may make me happy for a moment, but I know it would not have been God's best for me, and that's what we want, his best, not just good enough. It can get pretty painful to wait, but remember, it will be the best outcome because he sees everything that we don't.

Stop trying to figure everything out. Hang on and hang out for a while until you can see clearly where God is leading. Here are some suggestions while you wait:

† Stop talking, thinking, and replaying the problem over and over.

† Find something new, a purpose, while you wait.

† Surround yourself with encouraging, faith-building friends.

How many times have you gotten out ahead of yourself and found it made a mess? Take a moment to discuss. Remember, it's okay; we've all been there.

_____

_____

_____

_____

_____

_____

_____

_____

_____

_____

Beautiful truths to hold on to and claim this week:

I can live in my happy place when I am forgiven and walking in forgiveness.

God can change the direction of my thoughts.

I can have a happy place serving others.

*I can walk in peace knowing
that God has my back.*

*I can claim victory over any
situation because God loves me.*

Deep Thoughts and Reflections

Before moving on to the next chapter, spend some time thinking about what is currently holding you back from being truly happy, filled with joy, experiencing fulfillment, feeling loved and accepted (or what has done so in the past) and share your thoughts here.

_____

_____

_____

_____

_____

_____

How have these thoughts, feelings, or obstacles impacted your relationship with the Lord?

_____

_____

_____

_____

_____

_____

Remember, this exercise is for you only; no one else will see it, so be very honest with yourself. Jot down your thoughts and feelings here.

_____

_____

_____

_____

Thank goodness God sees
us, residue and all, and still pushes us
forward toward our destiny.

Chapter 3

I'm Not Going Back

Your extraordinary is just waiting to happen.

Jesus valued women more than you may realize. Many women opened their hearts to his ministry and were considered important enough to be a part of his inner circle. Did I say "inner circle"? Yes. The Bible mentions three women specifically in the book of Luke:

> He continued according to plan, traveled to town after town, village after village, preaching God's kingdom, spreading the Message. The Twelve were with him. There were also some women in their company who had been healed of various evil afflictions and illnesses: Mary, the one called Magdalene, from whom seven demons had gone out; Joanna, wife of Chuza, Herod's manager; and Susanna, along with many others who used their considerable means to provide for the company. (Luke 8:1–3 MSG)

These extraordinary women decided to support Jesus's ministry by traveling with him. No doubt, just as we have different personalities and life circumstances, they were giving their best while there. Now healed of evil spirits and diseases, these women had perhaps been previously overlooked in popular society or maybe they were possibly wealthy. Whatever the circumstance, Jesus thought enough of them to befriend them, heal them, and restore them to the joy of fellowship and service. This is a beautiful picture that illustrates for us that it doesn't matter where you come from, where you've been, or what you've done; you can be restored and share the great journey of serving well with God's women.

Ordinary woman can do extraordinary things for God.

For a long time, I thought I couldn't do anything important because I didn't have enough education and I wasn't pretty enough or as talented as others. I was wrong. God showed me the truths of his Word, and I can now do everything as a confident woman in ministry because I have been with Jesus.

> One of the Pharisees asked him over for a meal. He went to the Pharisee's house and sat down at the dinner table. Just then a woman of the village, the town harlot, having learned that Jesus was a guest in the home of the Pharisee, came with a bottle of very expensive perfume and stood at his feet, weeping, raining tears on his feet. Letting down her hair, she dried his feet, kissed them, and anointed them with the perfume. When the Pharisee who had invited him saw this, he said to himself, "If this man was the prophet I thought he was, he would have known what kind of woman this is who is falling all over him." (Luke 7:36–39 MSG)

Never is there a more celebrated moment than when Jesus meets a woman who is a disrespected outcast, known around town as a harlot. Mary is an uninvited guest to a dinner party. She carries with her a rare and beautiful gift. The host? Simon the Pharisee. No one from her part of town would dare darken the doorway of such a prestigious man, yet she entered his house with boldness and expectation. *There he is,* she may have thought as she scanned the room. Jesus, reclining at the table, legs stretched before him, enjoying conversation and food in mixed company. Overcome with emotion, she approaches and stands behind him for a minute. Eyes are glaring, wondering what she is up to and what she is doing there. As she kneels at his feet, thoughts and feelings begin to overwhelm as she is consumed by his beauty. Weeping now, she wipes the tears falling from her eyes onto his feet with her long luxurious hair as an act of humble washing. She offers him a most treasured sacrifice as she then anoints his feet with a rare and expensive oil. Simon is appalled. Who does she think she is? Who is this man, that he would allow such a woman to touch him?

Many times, on my journey, I too felt appalling judgment as I approached my Savior with a gift, only to be judged by others ("Who do you think you are?") for stepping out. Do you think ordinary Mary had to overcome these same accusations as she approached the King as an uninvited guest? Do you think Mary thought, *No way am I going back now?*

> Jesus said to him, "Simon, I have something to tell you."
>
> "Oh? Tell me."
>
> "Two men were in debt to a banker. One owed five hundred silver pieces, the other fifty. Neither of

them could pay up, and so the banker canceled both debts. Which of the two would be more grateful?"

Simon answered, "I suppose the one who was forgiven the most."

"That's right," said Jesus. Then turning to the woman, but speaking to Simon, he said, "Do you see this woman? I came to your home; you provided no water for my feet, but she rained tears on my feet and dried them with her hair. You gave me no greeting, but from the time I arrived she hasn't quit kissing my feet. You provided nothing for freshening up, but she has soothed my feet with perfume. Impressive, isn't it? She was forgiven many, many sins, and so she is very, very grateful. If the forgiveness is minimal, the gratitude is minimal." (Luke 7:40–47 MSG)

This act of a humble and repentant sacrifice was never more beautiful than when it intersected with love. I marvel at the boldness of Mary. She could have stood in the back or outside the door, waiting for someone to invite her in, but she was not turning back; she gave it her all. Her gratefulness for new life gave her the tenacity to boldly move forward, and hope kept her moving. Like Mary, some of us may not have had the best of circumstances or made the right choices; however, that does not exclude us from a beautiful life going forward.

What did Jesus do for Mary when Simon the Pharisee didn't approve?

_____

_____

_____

_____

Mary was loved with unconditional acceptance, and Jesus defended her before men. Likewise, Jesus will also defend us and accept us into his inner circle. We can go forward with confidence knowing we have a savior who cares and gives us a fresh start.

Recall a time when you may have taken a risk and stepped out to do something amazing in spite of your critics.

_____

_____

_____

_____

_____

_____

_____

In the blanks below, write out Jeremiah 31:3:

_____

_____

_____

_____

Thank goodness God sees us, residue and all, and still pushes us forward toward our destiny.

Let's take a look at someone else who was seen as unimportant and underestimated with much residue, but later, he was anointed to be king of Israel.

Read 1 Samuel 16:7. What specific thing did God *not* look for in the selection of a king?

_____

_____

_____

_____

In this passage of scripture, the prophet Samuel goes in search of the next king. King Saul has disobeyed God one time too many, and now, the Lord is ready to anoint a new leader. The next leader will be a very young man and will take the throne after many years of waiting.

Samuel arrives at Jesse's home to anoint the next king from a selection of good-looking sons. I'm sure before he left, he thought to look for someone who resembled the last king, someone tall and impressive, who looked like a king. But God had another plan. He told Samuel not to look for the obvious person and not to choose on appearance alone. God's choice would be the youngest with the least experience, because he saw something beautiful in David's heart.

*Sometimes we just need to be
still and give it to God.*

King David's anointing was an important event; however, it was many years before he took the throne. The anointing was done in secret.

> So as David stood there among his brothers, Samuel took the flask of oil he had brought and anointed David with the oil. And the Spirit of the Lord came powerfully upon David from that day on. (1 Samuel 16:13 NLT)

No one gave David a party or announced it at the next staff meeting. It wasn't on MSN, the news, or Facebook, and Samuel didn't send a tweet or post a picture of him and David about it the next day. Quite the opposite, in fact: Nothing was mentioned at all about it, and Samuel went back to Ramah. Just like that, in the quiet of the day and without fanfare, God anointed and approved of the heart of a king. David didn't have to try to be king or change his physical appearance to look the part. He didn't have to go to coaching sessions or conferences. He was faithful, a man after God's own heart, and that is all the Lord required of him up to this point.

It's hard to fathom that sometimes, we just need to be still and give it to God. We don't always have to do something in order to be noticed. We just need to be ourselves and keep our hearts right, and at the right time, we will emerge according to God's plan. In other words, something beautiful is about to happen.

> So be content with who you are, and don't put on airs. God's strong hand is on you; he'll promote you at the right time. Live carefree before God; he is most careful with you. (1 Peter 5:6–7 MSG)

What was required of King David at the time of Samuel's visit?

_____

What did God see no one else could see?

_____

God readied and taught David great things he would need in those years before he was ready for the big time.

Jackie's Story

Let's not run from these teachable moments; we need them. For me, one such teachable moment happened as I stepped into my first women's ministry opportunity. After some time of leading Bible studies and counseling women, I had the opportunity to host our first women's ministry speaker in the main sanctuary of our church. This was a big deal. We were expecting two hundred for the sanctuary conference. Our main speaker was a lovely woman who had written the book I happened to be teaching in my women's group. I was so proud to have her speak in our main church sanctuary. This was big.

I thought I would impress her by attempting to learn the names of her children to mention as part of her introduction. Yes, I know; you are already cringing. Women are anxiously awaiting her introduction, the lights are low with the expectations high, and when I introduce her, I mispronounce the name of her son. I call him "Celeb," as in a "celebrity," when in fact, his name is Caleb, like the Bible character (LOL). I had no idea I had even said it until she got up and corrected me, in front of everyone.

I could immediately feel the hot redness in my face as I sunk down in my seat, reeling from embarrassment. I know, you're thinking now is the time to run, hide, and never look back. It's moments like these you will wonder if you have what it takes. Don't turn back; it's just a learning moment God uses to make us better. The good thing that came out of it? I learned to take my time, check the facts, and not add anything to the speaker's bio unless they've given it to you.

Relax. Our hope is in God. The truth is, we all have those unguarded moments of imperfection. Did it mean the end of my ministry? Absolutely not. I went on to many good things later. We simply have to give ourselves a break and learn from our mistakes. Say this out loud: "Even if I make a mistake, I'm not looking or going back."

Mistakes do not define us. No, they only make us better and give us hope for the future. I know this because I've made a lot of them. Each time a weakness from the past tries to consume me, something rises up on the inside, and a determination to be better takes over. God comes to my defense and provides me with the hope I need to do something beautiful in and with my life.

Amber's Story

We must make up our minds that even in the midst of hard, embarrassing, even hopeless circumstances, we will not lose hope. Never become hopeless. Dictonary.com defines the word *hopeless* as "providing no hope; beyond optimism or hope; desperate." While this definition sounds depressing at best, I'd venture to say that at one time or another, we've all felt at the end of our rope, as if there's no hope in sight, no way out, desperate, even by life's circumstances that are beyond our control. Can you think of a time in your life when you felt hopeless? Can you picture it? Can you almost feel the hurt in your heart just thinking about it? Hold on to that feeling for a moment. That's exactly where I think the widow at Zarephath is when Elijah approaches her city upon God's instruction that a widow there would supply him with food. Upon arrival, Elijah sees the widow and immediately asks for a drink of water. She doesn't even get out of sight, and he also asks her for bread.

Here's where that gut-wrenching feeling I asked you to hold onto a few moments ago comes in; she responds, with such hopelessness, "As surely as the LORD your God lives [...] I don't have any bread—only a handful of flour in a jar and a little olive oil in a jug. I am gathering a few sticks to take home and make a meal for myself and my son, that we may eat it—and die" (1 Kings 17:12 NIV).

As we read about the widow, it's easy to equate her to the modern-day single mom. She had been left alone to care for her son in a time of severe hardship throughout her city. It seemed she had been merely surviving for quite a while and knew her time was up, as there was literally nothing left. Having been a single mom myself for several years, my heart broke as I read her story. Oh, how I could relate to her desperation as she uttered the words aloud that she'd known in her heart for quite some time.

For those of us who are mothers, I'm sure we all agree there is nothing we wouldn't give and no sacrifice we wouldn't make to be sure our children's needs are met. There were many times during my season of singleness when I had to scrape up enough money to buy a gallon of milk. Any spare change to be scavenged from beneath the seats of my car or behind the couch cushions had long since been found and spent. Although times were difficult, money was tight, and there was no room for extras, God never left us without the necessities we needed. Each and every time I was at the place of desperation, he would send an unexpected gift that would carry me to the next need, and so on.

The same was true of the widow. Just when she found herself completely hopeless, God sent Elijah to her with a promise of hope wrapped up in a test of faith. She was indeed faithful as she sacrificially used what should have been the last of her oil and flour to make a meal, not for herself or for her son, but for a complete stranger she'd only just met. Because she was faithful to the Lord's message sent through his prophet, he multiplied her gift and provided for her needs. When we come to the place of hopelessness, God wants us to walk in faith as we look to him to meet our needs.

> But those who hope in the Lord will renew their strength. They will soar on wings like eagles; they will run and not grow weary, they will walk and not be faint. (Isaiah 40:31 NIV)

There's a song by MercyMe I absolutely love called "In You." The very first line of the song says, "I put my hope in you. I lay my life in the palm of your hand. I'm constantly drawn to you, oh Lord, in ways I cannot comprehend."

Who are you placing your hope in? Give it to God; he's the only true hope when we feel hopeless.

Beautiful Moment

Share a time when putting your hope in the Lord made all the difference.

_____

_____

_____

_____

_____

_____

_____

_____

PART 2.

The Discovery

ONE
OF THE
AMAZING
MYSTERIES
OF OUR
FAITH-FILLED
LIFE
IS THAT WITH
GOD'S GRACE...

WE ARE ABLE
TO DO WHAT WE
CAN'T DO
ALONE

Chapter 4

I'm Not What I Used to Be

I'm not what I used to be, and I will find a safe place, one that makes me happy, contented, and brings joy to my spirit. A place where encouragement, inspiration, and new experiences happen daily. I am letting go of the hard stuff and embracing the simple things that make an ordinary day feel great.

Jackie Tinkler

It all starts with grace.

Amber's Story

The scene opens on a little country church in the middle of pretty much nowhere. The building, much as your mind's eye would imagine ... four walls making up a perfect rectangular shape with a traditional steeple atop. The color? White, of course, with stained glass windows adorning each side perfectly spaced apart and beautiful to look upon. To the left of the church, a family cemetery, made up of simple headstones dating back hundreds of years and sharing a common theme of names chiseled upon them. These pieces of stone represent generations of family all somehow related, by blood or through a lifetime of service to the same small church, where they were saved by the blood and, therefore, became family by choice. To the right of the church, long cement tables constructed years prior, where quite frequently the congregation would share dinner on the grounds or enjoy a homemade ice cream social or watermelon cutting, followed by hours of fellowshipping and watching the younger generation run and play.

While this may sound like a scene from an old movie, it was in fact the second home to my paternal grandparents, who we lovingly called Mamaw and Papaw and who I adored with every ounce of my being.

My sister and I spent most of our childhood summers on their family farm, which was made up of forty-plus acres located in Chunchula, Alabama. My grandparents were both very involved in the church; they were there every time the doors were opened (and a lot of the time when they weren't). Over the years, Mamaw played many roles, from church secretary and treasurer to being on pastor search committees and so on. For many years, she was *the* flower committee. I vividly recall her getting up super early Sunday mornings, going out to her beautifully manicured flower garden, and cutting fresh flowers to arrange a centerpiece that would be placed on the altar table that morning. Papaw was a deacon, which meant he did whatever was needed, including passing the plate during the offertory hymn and the ornate silver serving pieces when the Lord's Supper was observed.

During many a service, I recall the pastor saying, "Take out the hymnal from the pew in front of you and turn to page ..." The hymn of choice, "Amazing Grace! How Sweet the Sound." I can still see myself standing next to my Mamaw, listening to her belt out those words with all her heart and soul. She had a less-than-stellar singing voice, but the passion in which she sang about God's grace made it the sweetest sound I'd ever heard. It was obvious this beloved woman of God knew a thing or two about grace. Goodness knows she practiced much grace and forgiveness with me, my sisters, and our cousins on more occasions than I can count over those many summers spent in her care. But more than that, she made sure that we understood the words of that sacred hymn and the grace that our Savior extended to each of us as he willingly gave his life to save each of ours.

> Let us praise God for his glorious grace, for the free
> gift he gave us in his dear Son. (Ephesians 1:6 GNT)

Although I accepted Christ at a young age, it wasn't until well into my adult years that I fully grasped the true meaning of the word *grace* and became tenderly aware just how hard it can be to extend to others. In those moments, I am gently reminded of the amazing grace that was so freely given to me thousands of years ago by a God who loved me so very much that he was willing to give his only Son so that I might receive grace for my sins. I know I will never be asked to give more grace to another than that.

My precious Mamaw went to be with the Lord in May of 2010. Her funeral was held in that same little country church that watched me grow from a young child into an adult and mother of two. "Amazing Grace" was one of the hymns sung during her service. As I joined in to sing this favorite hymn of hers, I couldn't help but wish she was standing right there next to me, belting out those words we had all come to know by heart to the Father she so faithfully served until her last breath. To this day, I can't hear "Amazing Grace" without thinking of my Mamaw and that little church. From her amazing example, I strive each day to show grace; what a legacy to leave behind. He has given it to us. All we have to do is pass it along.

But to each one of us grace has been given as Christ apportioned it. (Ephesians 4:7 NIV)

I may have been down, but I'm getting back up!!!

One of the amazing mysteries of our faith-filled life is that with God's grace, we are able to do what we can't do alone. When I hit a wall and can't find it within myself to perform, be, or do, I'm in my best place, because where I am weak, he is strong. It is just another opportunity for God's favor and power to be seen in my life. Only he can save a life when we come to him with our brokenness.

We may be underestimated and underrated but we're not finished yet, God Has More

Now you've got my feet on the life path, all radiant from the shining of your face. Ever since you took my hand, I'm on the right way. (Psalm 16:11 MSG)

Jackie's Story

I drove into the parking lot at the theatre, not knowing how this first meeting would go. We were meeting that day with the executive director and his technical staff to talk about an idea. I couldn't get this crazy idea out of my head. I was shown a little black box theatre off the main, which held around one hundred and fifty people, at the most. It was pitch-black as I walked into the room that day, knowing I was in over my head, but it felt just right. The warmth of the air and the cozy feel of velvet drapes and the tiny stage took me back to backstage jitters, rehearsals, and costumes as a kid. God reminded me that the dream was not over. I was sold on this location.

What if we could produce a local women's conference at some of the best theatres right here in town? It could be a theatrical production and conference all in one, which would enable us to show the love of Jesus and inspire women to connect to a better life through music, dance, worship, and great local speakers.

In 2004, *Transformation* happened in that little black box theatre at the King Center in Melbourne, Florida. For the next four years, *Transformation* happened for over four hundred women in small theatres across Brevard County, as an annual conference and place to celebrate new life.

But God had another plan for me. During the economic crisis of 2008, we ran out of money for the production. The conference would have to wait and, needless to say, my heart was broken and confused. God told me, "Wait, let it go for now, and as you wait, we'll work on the transformation of you." Not what I wanted to hear. I was devastated. How could this happen? I had no earthly idea I would have to wait years before I could dream a new dream. I know, big sigh.

As I went through an extended time of growth, personally and vocationally, my faith in my dream grew dim. I began to lose hope; other people forgot the dream and thought I was done. How many of us feel that way right now? We tried to do everything we knew to do, but our dreams of being healed or having a great marriage, a child, a new career, or early retirement didn't happen the way we thought it would. There were serious questions in my mind as to why God would allow my heart to be broken like this. Why was it taking so long for God to do something? Do I ever get it, girls.

What I didn't know was that God had something better for me, in a place I never knew existed. God was working something beautiful out of my pain, and he would use it to do a new thing. During that wait, he worked out a lot of things in me for larger capacity than I ever thought. As I healed from the disappointment of that time, God made something beautiful from the ashes.

I know what it is to be left on the back burner for a long time. We wonder if God is ever going to come rescue our broken heart.

Isaiah had prophesied years before Jesus was born that someone was coming to give beauty in return for broken hearts.

> And provide for those who grieve in Zion, to bestow on them a crown of beauty instead of ashes, the oil of joy instead of mourning, and a garment of praise instead of a spirit of despair. They will be called oaks of righteousness, a planting of the LORD for the display of his splendor. (Isaiah 61:3 NIV)

What three things does God promise in return for a broken heart?

FOR

_____   _____

INSTEAD
OF

_____   _____

INSTEAD
OF

_____   _____

Share if you are disappointed, discouraged, or just plain tired. Tell God how you feel.

_____

_____

_____

_____

Dear ladies, God walks us through our difficult times. He wants to lead us by his very still small voice. When we are restless, tired, bored, angry, or worn, it's difficult to hear or see anything good about our circumstances. Know that God wants the best to come from hard times. Begin to speak and believe the best possible outcome.

Write out Romans 8:31 here and speak it out loud.

_____

_____

_____

_____

Be filled with a blessing of wellness, friends. We have an enemy who would love to steal our faith. He wants us to believe that we will have to live in the mess we made. Beautiful girl, we don't have to. Our something beautiful is coming; the mess and its craziness will be redeemed, and we will be planted by God in a special place where people will say, "Wow, look what God did." Promise.

Father, help us to see you in the mess and know that you would never desire us to stay in our circumstances, but to thrive. You are our constant source of happiness and joy. Thank you for leading us to that special place of promise. Each promise is unique and different and made just for how you made us. Help us to grow into that promise feeling powerful and assured of a good future.

Jackie's Story

Recently, my family and I were in Florida for my daughter Lauren's college graduation. We went out for dinner after graduation and then strolled the cobblestone streets filled with unique boutiques and shops in St. Augustine. There is a quaint little park in the middle of the median going through King Street, and on this evening, vendors and crafters set up booths. A colorful booth caught my eye with its beautiful display of handcrafted handbags. As I fought past the crowded display, I smelled the slight aroma of tire rubber, which was odd, but I was already in love with the black bag and its beautiful rose imprint painted in red on the front flap, so no going back now. The bag was well made and beautiful. I couldn't stop looking at it and thought it was uniquely special. The vendor explained that these exquisite purses were actually made from the repurposed rubber of a car tire. What? A used tire, remade into something useful and attractive; a work of art.

Just like that handbag made from rubber, we are not what we used to be. We are a beautiful recreation: unique, rare, and exquisite.

Beautiful Moment

Read 2 Corinthians 5:16–17 and 2 Corinthians 10:4.

We all want to live the beautiful life; what are the two things the war in our minds produce that keep us from receiving it?

1. _____

2. _____

As you can see, our thinking keeps us from really knowing the love of God and allowing the light of his beauty in.

So here's what I want you to do, God helping you: Take your everyday, ordinary life—your sleeping, eating, going-to-work, and walking-around life—and place it before God as an offering. Embracing what God does for you is the best thing you can do for him. Don't become so well-adjusted to your culture that you fit into it without even thinking. Instead, fix your attention on God. You'll be changed from the inside out. Readily recognize what he wants from you, and quickly respond to it. Unlike the culture around you, always dragging you down to its level of immaturity, God brings the best out of you, develops well-formed maturity in you. (Romans 12:2 MSG)

Personally, girlfriends, I was tired of being a confused, fearful, and emotional Christian with no power. It was only *after* I found my way to some faith-builders, encouragers, and mentors, and studied the Word, that my thinking changed. It was then that I found purpose.

Write out the following additional scriptures for inspiration:

Philippians 4:13:

_____

_____

_____

_____

_____

Proverbs 3:5–6

_____

_____

_____

_____

_____

Jeremiah 29:11

_____

_____

_____

_____

Ephesians 1:18

_____

_____

_____

_____

_____

On a final note, write down some of the things you would like to celebrate going forward. Share them with your girlfriends now. We want to celebrate with you.

_____

_____

_____

_____

_____

_____

_____

_____

66

The making
of a beauty
comes
through
challenges and
pressure
mixed
with His
perfect timing
and grace

Chapter 5

I'm Finding the Real Me

I dream of a place where being my true self is not a struggle. It's that place where frustration melts away and the hope of another day begins.

Jackie Tinkler

Amber's Story

How many times have you gone to a concert, watched a movie, attended a major sporting event, or been anywhere in the presence of a true celebrity, and thought, *I sure wish I was famous, that everyone knew me just by seeing my face or hearing my name*? Anyone saying yes right now or raising your hand? Yeah, me too.

For me, this kind of thinking started as early as my carefree days in the K4 class at Ridgecrest Baptist. Kindergarten wasn't real school, so we didn't have assignments, per se, but we did lots of coloring projects. I remember one of these projects so vividly. The teacher gave each student two coloring sheets: one had three ducks on it and the other a pond. The assignment was first color the pond and then color the ducks, cut them out, and paste them on the pond. As my classmates began gluing their ducks flat on their ponds, I thought to myself, *Here's my chance to be noticed. How can I stand out?*

Well, for starters, their ducks were pasted flat on their pond sheet. Rather than floating, they looked more like they were drowning. I quickly came up with the idea of folding a small crease at the bottom of each duck and pasting only that part to the pond. The result? My ducks were actually floating on the pond. Yes, I was a control freak even then, but the teacher thought it was brilliant, and thus began my desire to be known.

This desire came from a place deep inside me, where there was a hole that I never could seem to fill.

My parents divorced when I was just a toddler, and my father wasn't exactly active in my life, as he lived in a different state and had another family. I longed to have the daddy/daughter relationship so many of my friends had and I saw on every movie and TV show I watched. Sadly, this longing was never fulfilled. High school came, and I so deeply desired to be part of the popular crowd; although I was in the top sorority on campus and had many friends, most of those friendships were only within the walls of the school. I was never asked out, so I didn't date until my senior year. I refused to go to my sorority formal again without a date, so I asked a guy I thought was cute. He said yes; we went, had a great time, and saw each other for a few months after, but it never amounted to much, and the hole remained. Shortly after high school, I met a guy; we dated, fell in love, and got married. Finally, someone actually knew me. The newlywed stage wore off, and that hole still longed to be filled. Children came, and although to this day they are my greatest joy in life, there was still something missing. My marriage ended after sixteen years, and the hole became a crater.

During this season, when I felt I'd hit rock bottom and was all alone, the Lord began to speak to me about my true identity. Guess what I finally realized? My identity wasn't in having the best duck picture (although it was amazing, especially for a kindergartner), and it wasn't about finding a husband or even making a home with beautiful children. My true identity is in Christ. Regardless of the lies the enemy hoped I'd continue to believe, I am famous, famous in my heavenly Father's eyes. He made me, he knows me, and he loves me just the way I am.

> But whoever loves God is known by God.
> (1 Corinthians 8:3 NIV)

And the best news of all? This is true for you as well. So on those hard days when you're feeling like you don't quite measure up, you need look no further than above because you, sweet sister, are *known* by your heavenly Father. Say this sentence out loud and claim it over your life every day:

"My name is [fill in the blank], and I am known by God."

Read this beautiful passage from Psalm 139 aloud with your small group girlfriends!

> You made all the delicate, inner parts of my body and knit me together in my mother's womb. Thank you for making me so wonderfully complex! Your workmanship is marvelous—how well I know it. You watched me as I was being formed in utter seclusion, as I was woven together in the dark of the womb. You saw me before I was born. Every day of my life was recorded in your book. Every moment

was laid out before a single day had passed. (Psalm 139:13–16 NLT)

How many days did God plan ahead of time for you?

_____

Read Genesis 1:27–28.

For what beautiful purpose did God create you?

1. _____

_____

2. _____

_____

God has always had you in mind from the creation of the earth as a contributor, an heir, and a servant. We were not born just to exist in the world. We believe every one of us is an absolute jewel to God with a purpose to know him, enjoy life, serve others, and invite them to know the Lord too.

Now that's beautiful!

According to Jeremiah 29:11, what is God's spiritual direction for your life?

1. _____

_____

2. _____

_____

3. _____

_____

4. _____

_____

God has a good and beautiful plan for our lives. It is his plan, regardless of the haters and negative-speaking people in your life. It is still his plan, even when you doubt it or don't see it. When we can't pay the rent, our marriage is crumbling, people use us, or our dreams aren't coming true, it is still his plan. His hands made and created you. How in the world can another person on this planet know more about you than God?

Along the path to something beautiful, we as women, love to talk and ask for opinions. But too many opinions, especially wrong opinions, can be confusing. We need only two or three close, trustworthy, and safe friends who will tell us the truth in love. We trust them because we can see stability and life coming from them. Don't get fooled into a false sense of security with people who are not ready to speak into our lives in a loving, positive way. I love the book *Safe People* by Dr. Henry Cloud and Dr. John Townsend. People are a part of our journey, but not everyone will help to nurture our walk with God. In order to grow, we need someone safe and faithful to count on.

According to Cloud and Townsend, when asked to describe a "safe person," people gave the following descriptions:

† a person who accepts me just as I am

† a person who loves me no matter how I am being or what I do

† someone who gives me an opportunity to grow

In my younger days, I would talk to anyone and everyone about my problems. You guessed it: I invited in a lot of trouble and drama, and before I knew it, I was handing over my heart on a plate. I just didn't know how to recognize someone safe.

Clothe Yourself with What Matters.

Amber's Story

When I hear the word *clothed* today, lots of things come to my mind. Interestingly, however, my thoughts have differed quite substantially over the years where the meaning of this word is concerned.

As a young child, being clothed simply meant that I had some sort of article of clothing on my body and wasn't running around the house, fresh out of the tub, wearing only my birthday suit. In those days, it didn't matter if I matched, had holes in my shoes, was wearing muddy play clothes, or sported my Sunday best; clothes were just that: clothes.

As I grew and became a teenager, being clothed no longer meant just throwing something on. Oh no, everything had to match. And the brand name; yes, it mattered, a lot. I would search high and low for the in brands and styles: Guess jeans, Reebok high-tops, super-white Keds, a black Members Only jacket, and at least two or three Swatch watches were a must for any kid of the 1980s.

When I entered adulthood, the brand didn't seem to matter so much, and I quickly became a pro at dressing myself nice on a fairly limited budget. A few years after I married, babies came, and clothing them reached a whole new level of insanity. It suddenly became acceptable to grab whatever was on sale or looked halfway decent for me so that my little ones could be dressed to the nines. It was an absolute must that they always look undeniably adorable; monograms and smocking? Yes, please. I was willing to make any sacrifice necessary to ensure my children were taken care of and had the best of everything, including clothes.

As my children grew, the importance of dressing them in the latest and greatest began to take a back seat to ensuring they were clothed with the truths of God's Word. Dressing them up was so much fun, but their salvation and a personal relationship with the Lord was imperative.

Just as my Father longed for many years to clothe me in his righteousness, I too wanted that for my children. Isn't it funny how our priorities change when we become mothers and begin to see through our heavenly Father's eyes to gain a little bit of perspective? I rejoiced as I had the privilege of witnessing each of my children profess Christ as their Savior and make it public through a baptismal experience.

> I delight greatly in the Lord; my soul rejoices in my God. For he has clothed me with garments of salvation and arrayed me in a robe of his righteousness, as a bridegroom adorns his head like a priest and as a bride adorns herself with her jewels. (Isaiah 61:10 NIV)

My children are now young adults, making their own decisions and blazing their own paths in life. I praise him each day that they are his. *Clothed* today has a whole new meaning for me, as my focus in this season of life is walking out a godly example daily, not only before my children but also before each person the Lord has placed in my path. There are many days I feel I fall short of the mark;

however, it's in those moments the Lord gently reminds me that I am created in his image. When I said yes to his knock at my heart's door, I was instantly covered with the veil of his blood so that I can stand blameless before God. This fact is true for each and every believer, and although we may not feel we are righteous, virtuous, or dressed to the nines, we can rest assured that Jesus went to the cross for each one of us so we could be clothed in his righteousness and holiness.

Walk confidently today in the assurance that you are perfect in your Father's eyes, and wear your crown like the princess you are, worthy of the calling he has placed before you, clothed with strength and dignity, just as his Word proclaims.

Inevitably, the path to something beautiful will have a hard day, here and there. When we encounter those tough moments, don't give up. The hard days are part of our growth and beauty routine.

These experiences try your patience, enhance your endurance, and develop your maturity. We can trust him through the trial or give up and take the path of least resistance, but I won't look as beautiful if I don't allow God to refine me. Say this out loud: "It's only temporary."

Let me suggest a change in attitude, a quiet trust, and a determined patience while we wait on the Lord for the outcome. Luke 21:19 (NIV) says, "Stand firm, and you will win life."

List below the beautiful attributes of a hardship or trial:

_____

_____

_____

Consider it a sheer gift, friends, when tests and challenges come at you from all sides. You know that under pressure, your faith life is forced into the open and shows its true colors. So don't try to get out of anything prematurely. Let it do its work so you become mature and well-developed, not deficient in any way. (James 1:2–4 MSG)

It is in the delicate moments of pressure we find our best self. Why the pressure? It...

† matures us,

† takes time,

† ensures success,

† is an investment into our future,

† is complete and not lacking, and

† fine-tunes our character.

The making
of a beauty
comes
through
challenges
and
pressure
mixed with
his perfect
timing and
grace.

Jackie's Story

I used to think things should come easily. If it got too hard, it was easy to just give up and move on to something else. So whenever something got hard, I would quit. The problem here is that I missed the opportunity to grow. No one likes the hard days, but they are necessary because they make us more beautiful, like Jesus. Jesus walked a hard road to Calvary to give up his life for you and me. His sacrifice was like a sweet perfume, and although hard, something beautiful came from it.

Our character is an important foundation to our beauty, where God invites us to be ready for the future.

Read Mark 4:35–41. In the New Living Translation, it says "a bad storm came up." Isn't that the way it happens? It just comes up, from what seems like out of nowhere. You weren't looking for it or asking for it. And Jesus is sleeping? Hello? Whenever my husband and I are in the car together and it's been awhile since he's said anything to me, I look over and say, "Hello? I'm here." So there is Jesus asleep in the back of the boat on a pillow, I imagine very tired. If it was me, I would adjust my duvet, sheets, and pillows just right (building my nest), before I drift off to sleep, and if anything disturbs me in that process, I'm not a happy camper. Well, here comes Jesus's wake-up call after he just got settled. His disciples are going nuts in a personal storm. Very afraid, they screamed, "Hey, Jesus, we're in trouble here; help us. We are going to die; don't you care?" And this is exactly how we feel: panicked and afraid. We wonder why God doesn't do something about our crisis.

> He got up, rebuked the wind and said to the waves, "Quiet! Be still!" Then the wind died down and it was completely calm." (Mark 4:39 NIV)

Jesus intended on helping all along, but, listen carefully here, our commotion drowns out his still small voice.

When the noise and commotion of any personal storm begins to rattle your boat, it's time for your mouth, thoughts, and actions to be quiet so you can hear God. Refrain from rehearsing the problem or speaking about it to anyone who will listen. Often the winds and waves are the sounds of too many voices. Settle down; the peace will come. It's the fear in us that causes all the craziness. Once we can get past the fear, call peace over our household, and hear God's voice, we are then able to make wise and sound decisions.

Share about a time God made something beautiful from a personal storm of your past.

_____

_____

_____

_____

_____

_____

How did you grow spiritually?

_____

_____

_____

_____

_____

Beautiful Moment

How can you find a happy place in the midst of the storm? Here are a few suggestions:

- Get quiet and be at peace.

- Pray more, talk less.

- Get perspective.

- Change what you can, and let God have the rest.

- Have reasonable expectations.

- Don't put too much pressure on yourself or others to give us what only God can.

- Create a place of safety, comfort, and warmth in your home.

- Find a place where you can relax, play, and live free from stress.

- Get involved in a life-giving group or Bible study.

Make a list of three simple things that make you happy:

1. _____

_____

2. _____

_____

3. _____

PURE JOY DOESN'T *come from* A PERSON, A POSSESSION, OR EVEN A POSITIVE LIFE *circumstance;* IT COMES FROM *giving and investing in* THINGS THAT *are eternal.*

Chapter 6

I Have a Happy Place

When I'm in my "happy place," a stillness and calm
wash over me. It's hard to put the feeling into words,
but I liken it to being in the presence of the Lord;
it's peaceful, serene, beautiful.

Amber Edwards

Amber's Story

What makes you happy? When I'm asked this question, a thousand
things flood my mind, various things, both large and small, that
make me smile and give me a happy high in the moment. I begin to
see with my mind's eye a warm chocolate chip cookie fresh out of the
oven (well, anything chocolate, really), brunch at a trendy restaurant
with my precious group of girlfriends, a romantic candlelight dinner
with my hubby, sitting on the beach under a beautiful blue sky; put
me in any one of these scenarios, and yes, I'm a happy girl. But what
happens when the chocolate is gone or the trip is over? Is the feeling
of happiness still there?

For far too many years, I struggled with finding true and
lasting happiness. Although I accepted Christ at a young age, a

lot of life's circumstances seemed to keep me, well, looking at life's circumstances. Shortly after my extremely hard marriage of sixteen years ended in a devastating divorce, my precious Mamaw passed away. I found myself in a season where I was a broke, single mom, parenting two kids who were devastated by the separation and struggling to understand why their parents were no longer living under the same roof. Add in a few years of dating in a world where dating was no longer just dinner and a movie, and all of this resulted in long bouts of loneliness. It seemed there was no joy to be had; happiness had completely evaded me.

All that changed in January 2011, when it hit me like a lead balloon that I had to stop looking to my circumstances to make me happy; I must look to my Savior. That year, I decided things were going to change and I was turning over my circumstances to the Lord. I remember praying, "Lord, if this is what you have for me, if being a single mom is your plan for my life, make that the desire of my heart." Later that month, I met an amazing man who is now my husband and a wonderful father to my children.

Now I'm not saying that God gave me a man, and that made everything instantly better. But I have no doubt the Lord placed Michael in my life for a reason. His unconditional love and constant encouragement allowed me to finally see past my circumstances. For the first time in my adult life, I had a partner who truly believed I could do anything I set my mind to. He supported me in every new venture I set out to undertake. I felt beyond blessed, and my heart yearned to share that feeling with others who may be hurting or need some encouragement as well.

Early in 2012, I felt the Lord speaking to me about serving others. Now, this had always been a desire of my heart and something I longed to do, but never before had I felt the support or means to do it. I had no idea where to even begin, but the Lord was telling me to do something, and I was bursting at the seams to make a difference, no matter how large or small. That year, our family set out on an evening of performing random acts of kindness. It was so much fun. From that point on, it took off, and we began serving people as a family in many various ways, both large and small. Guess what I finally learned and found? Joy. There is nothing that brings me more happiness or greater joy than doing something for someone else, especially someone who is hurting or in need. God finally revealed to me that happiness—I mean pure joy—doesn't come from a person, a possession, or even a positive life circumstance; it comes from giving and investing in things that are eternal, in serving God's creations.

> Each of you should use whatever gift you have received to serve others, as faithful stewards of God's grace in its various forms. (1 Peter 4:10 NIV)

Are you seeking happiness or a true sense of joy? Try helping or serving someone else, a complete stranger, even. I promise you: the blessing will be all yours and not only in that moment, but throughout eternity.

If someone were to ask you, "What makes you happy?" what would your answer be? Before reading further, take a few moments to jot down the first few things that come to your mind in the space below:

_____

_____

_____

_____

_____

_____

_____

_____

_____

Here are a few of ours:

Amber	*Jackie*
Unsweet tea with LOTS of ice	A HOT cup of coffee
Freshly baked chocolate chip cookies (*or anything chocolate, really!*)	Sharing the end of the day with my hubby
Sleeping late or napping	Strolling through an antique mall
Date night with my hubby	Spending time with my girlfriends
A nice, thick pair of fuzzy socks	Playing dress-up
Brunch with my girlfriends	Giving my dog a hug
Quality time with my little fam of four	Hearing the voice of God
Attending church or praise and worship time	Listening or dancing to nostalgic music from the 1970s

Any and all of these things will most certainly bring a smile to our faces and make our hearts happy in the moment; however, what about after the moment is gone? What happens when we get down to the bare bones, and it's just us, alone and quiet? Some of you may be saying, "'Alone' or 'quiet'? Those words don't even exist in my world," and sister, we get it. I'm talking about when everything is stripped away, and it's just you, alone with your thoughts. Is your spirit truly happy? Close your eyes for a moment, and allow your mind's eye to picture a time when you were truly at peace. What does that look like? For me, it's carefree days of summer spent at my Mamaw's house, hanging out with my cousins, dancing in the rain, stomping through mud puddles, and so on. For Jackie, it's sitting around the large table in her grandmother's kitchen as a child.

The apostle Paul had a happy place. He shared these words about that place for him in the book of Philippians:

> Therefore, my dear brothers and sisters, stay true to the Lord. I love you and long to see you, dear friends, for you are my joy and the crown I receive for my work. (Philippians 4:1 NLT)

It wasn't easy for Paul, but it was worth living his life for others.

How does Paul describe his friends? They are his _____ and _____.

What kind of life is a rewarding life? _____

_____

Take a look at James 1:12 and write it here:

_____

_____

_____

_____

Fix Your Thoughts on Rightful Living ...

Our thoughts really do lead us in the direction we want to go.

And now, dear brothers and sisters, one final thing. Fix your thoughts on what is true, and honorable, and right, and pure, and lovely, and admirable. Think about things that are excellent and worthy of praise. Keep putting into practice all you learned and received from me—everything you heard from me and saw me doing. Then the God of peace will be with you. (Philippians 4:8–9 NLT)

What does the scripture tell us to do in order to think the way God thinks?

_____

_____

Don't worry about anything; instead, pray about everything. Tell God what you need, and thank him for all he has done. Then you will experience God's peace, which exceeds anything we can understand. His peace will guard your hearts and minds as you live in Christ Jesus. (Philippians 4:6–7 NLT)

What guards our hearts and minds as we think happy thoughts?

_____

_____

It's not only good therapy to get your mind off your problems; it's also essential for living out something beautiful. God made us to be with one another, and he emphasizes this throughout scripture.

> Two are better than one, because they have a good return for their labor: If either of them falls down, one can help the other up. But pity anyone who falls and has no one to help them up. Also, if two lie down together, they will keep warm. But how can one keep warm alone? Though one may be overpowered, two can defend themselves. A cord of three strands is not quickly broken. (Ecclesiastes 4:9–12 NIV)

In his infinite wisdom, even looking ahead to generations yet to come, the Lord knew how important our friendships would be, especially to us as women. But he also knew how busy we would become. Let's be honest, ladies; we're living in an age of to-do lists, and we're constantly being challenged by those around us to be everything to everybody. We spend our days running from one thing to the next but never really enjoying anything because we're so worried about fitting it all in. We fall into bed each night, hoping to catch a few hours' sleep, but before we drift off, we've already made our mental list of tomorrow's demands.

We've been pushed to the point where letting something go isn't an option; it's a necessity. Many times as adults, that something is our friends. Of course, this is not intentional, nor does it happen overnight, but it does happen. We start working, maybe get married and have a couple of kids, and suddenly, we become overwhelmed. For some of us, our schedules begin to dictate our days and who we spend them with. Phone calls to catch up with friends have been replaced by a quick scroll through social media and the click of a "like" button, which we convince ourselves shows our friends that we are interested and involved in what's actually going on in their world. And if we read of a tragedy, we may squeeze in a few seconds to type a quick "I'm praying for you."

We challenge each of you reading this to spend some time this week reaching out to a friend, perhaps someone you haven't spoken with in quite a while. And don't stop there; carve out time in your schedule each week to show someone you care. Make friendship a priority in your life once again, instead of an option. Let's be the generation who models God's definition of friendship so well that it becomes the standard for everyone around us, everyone around them, and so on.

Jot down the name of a friend or two (or three or four) who you adore, but because of life's circumstances, you rarely get to talk to, much less see and spend time with:

_____

_____

_____

_____

_____

_____

_____

_____

_____

_____

_____

Think of a few ways you can be more intentional in reaching out to these friends and showing them you care. Share your thoughts here:

_____

_____

_____

_____

_____

_____

_____

_____

PART 3.

The Beautiful Life

"

If we stay
where we are,
then we
haven't stepped
out in faith in
the direction
of...

SOMETHING
MORE

Chapter 7

I Expect More

We're not stuck in the way things were.

Jackie's Story

Looking back, it was a hot day, riding in the backseat of my parents' GTO, with the windows rolled down and the wind pleasantly blowing in my face. *This is going to be a great day,* I thought to myself. I was all of eight, and my entire family (parents, grandmothers, friends, cousins, brothers, and sisters) and I traveled in three separate cars, making our way to sunny Florida out of the gray skies and dirty snow of Upstate New York. My dream of going to Disney was about to happen, and the excitement would build each time my parents would say, "We're almost there." It seemed everything about that trip was heaven: an unending happy day. I can remember taking my own daughter for the first time many, many years later, her little face lighting up at each new adventure. I have pictures of Goofy holding Lauren in the air as her feet dangled in delight.

These are the happy Disney moments of life, but there is more yet to be discovered. Disney World and its experience of being "the happiest place on earth" can't compare with what God has in store for us. I know that is hard to imagine.

God's love is more than the sun shining all day or the warm, balmy breeze felt blowing in my hair. It's more refreshing than that cool dip in the pool and even the beautiful amber sunset of a perfect night. God's laughter is the most brilliant sound you could ever hear, and his whisper is like the soothing sound of a waterfall. He *is* more.

We were never created to settle...

Once we find contentment in God, we will have more than we could ever dream.

Yes. We can have more, according to his power that is at work within us. He gives us a burst of something beautiful to accomplish more than we thought we could.

Write Ephesians 3:19 here:

_____

_____

_____

_____

"Know" in the Greek means "*to know by experience.*"

What has your relationship with God been like up until now? Has he been a good Father? Has he been distant, disconnected, and unattached? Write your feelings here, and give yourself permission to be honest:

_____

_____

_____

_____

_____

Our prayer is that we come to "know this love that surpasses knowledge—that you may be filled to the measure of all the fullness of God" (Ephesians 3:19 NIV).

What are we being filled with, dear ones? Are you full to the top with his can-do power, his incredible push through determination?

Now, if we could only let go of self so we can be filled with something beyond ourselves. Our relationship with Jesus makes this possible. Let's give our hopes, dreams, and the something beautiful to him and see what he makes it: more than we have the capacity to hold. God is working beyond what we think, because our thinking is limited to the world we live in.

Read Ephesians 3:20 and write it here in your own words:

_____

_____

_____

_____

Now read this same verse from the Message translation of God's Word:

> God can do anything, you know ...far more than
> you could ever imagine or guess or request in

your wildest dreams! He does it not by pushing us around, but by working within us, his Spirit deeply and gently within us. (Ephesians 3:20 MSG)

What are the current limits that keep you from believing God can do something beautiful in your life? Share them here:

_____

_____

_____

_____

_____

_____

If anything was possible, what would you need to accomplish your something beautiful? Share your thoughts here:

_____

_____

_____

_____

_____

_____

Why not invite God's Word into your daily routine?

I sense there are a lot of us girls out there looking for more than we are currently experiencing. We want something beautiful but don't quite know how to get there or even how to define it. Maybe some of us have been in crisis mode, making a living and getting by for so long that we've forgotten how to dream. Limits can be self-imposed, placed on us by others or just tough circumstances. The challenge is seeing our limits through the truth of God's Word.

If we were sitting together right now enjoying coffee, we would pray for God to take those limits off by showing you how to be filled with more of him to overcome anything.

Get going girl!

We can do anything he wills for us

With the right timing, a little faith, and plenty of love, we are on our way to something beautiful.

One thing you can be certain of if you're going to expect more is that there will be a change. God may even ask you to change a little.

Jackie's Story

Change is good. We recently experienced a big change moving to Birmingham, Alabama. Being Florida natives and never moving outside of our beachy, breezy hometown of Melbourne, you can pretty much say we experienced culture shock. God had better things for us. He gave us a little push after a job loss, and here we are. If we hadn't had the push, I'm fairly certain we would not have had this adventure. Yes. It was uncomfortable to be new and navigate a big city. Was it crazy that everyone knew us in our home church in Melbourne, and we had to start over in a new church? Yes, it was. Was it scary to start over again in our forties and fifties? Yes, it was, but God was at the center of it, and although it may have been uncomfortable, it wasn't long before our feet were planted in this bigger than life place, and we were happy again.

Some of us will love the adventure of change, and some of us would rather go back to bed and throw the covers over our head. Here is the thing: God never expects us to stay where we are. After having a few decades under our belts, we've learned that things never stay the same. It's when we refuse to budge, we get stuck. If we're going to expect more, then we'll need to expect it will come by change.

Change... That thing that happens when something is over.

If we stay where we are, then we haven't stepped out in faith in the direction of something more.

Where I am currently:

_____

_____

_____

_____

_____

_____

Where I want to go:

_____

_____

_____

_____

_____

Are you willing to do something different to have more?

_____

_____

_____

_____

_____

Let's Pray Together

Amazing Father, we want to know you more, deepen our fellowship, and watch you do the more in our lives, the exceedingly, abundantly beautiful. Give us the ability to understand the "far more" you have for us. Do what we can't do. Surprise us, Lord. Surprise us beyond our wildest dreams and expectations. Go above our thinking. We're waiting, Lord, for something beautiful to happen that we never expected.

Love,

_____

[Sign your name here]

Deep Thoughts and Reflections

As women, we tend to do a lot and try to be strong for ourselves, our family, and our friends. It takes patience and trust to wait on God to fix what's wrong. We often feel exhausted. Perhaps we need a change of perspective. Think of the things you love to do that truly give you rest and write them here. Look at this list next time you need a reminder that you can enjoy, and God's got it.

_____

_____

_____

_____

_____

_____

_____

Here are a few of ours:

Cozy up with a good book

Turn off the noise

Put up white lights
on the back porch

Gaze at the stars

Light a candle

Quiet time with family

Spend some time with
a good friend

Enjoy a nice breakfast

Read God's Word

Stretch

Spend fifteen minutes
in the sun

Take deep breaths

Talk to God

Take a hot bubble bath

God
has
an
amazing
plan
for
your
life,
but...

you have to be willing to say "not my will Lord, but yours"

I'm Ready to Dream Big

A dream is no longer just a wish when we hand it
over to God because if it's his will, it will be done.
Anything is possible with God.

Amber Edwards

When you hear the word *dream*, what immediately comes to your
mind? What dreams have you been hiding deep in your heart?
Maybe they seem completely out of reach, even impossible, so you've
pushed them deep down because the enemy has convinced you
there's absolutely no way those dreams could ever become reality
for you.

If you could do anything, absolutely anything, without
consideration of any outside factor (money, time, etc.), if you could
live your perfect life, walk out your dream, what would that look
like for you? Jot down a few thoughts here:

_____

_____

Amber's Story

For years, I've dreamed of being my own boss and running my own nonprofit company, not just any business, but something that brings joy to others. I've stepped out towards this dream more times than I care to mention. I've walked in so many different endeavors, and at the time, I really felt like the Lord was leading me down that particular path. I had a catering business that allowed me to work with all different types of people: brides on their big day, couples celebrating milestone anniversaries, first-time moms celebrating their precious gift from above, and the list goes on. I had a gift basket business where I created beautiful baskets with handpicked items that I knew would bring a huge smile to the face of the recipient. I made crafts to sell at different craft fairs around the state. I had my own makeup and skincare business, and so on and so forth. I put my heart and soul into each one of these endeavors, and I was truly passionate about the people I was touching, but none of these ventures ever endured. At the end of the day, I found myself disappointed again and again.

Why wasn't anything working? Why wasn't God blessing my efforts? God had gifted me with all these amazing talents, and I was trying to use them, but nothing seemed to be working out. Why? This question rang in my mind for years, but all the while, he kept molding and shaping me, and I kept feeling in my spirit that there was something bigger, a larger purpose; he had something more for me.

When I least expected it and through his divine plan, I met a precious new friend through a small group. We immediately clicked. We got to know each other more and more, and we began to realize that the dreams we had in our hearts were very similar. As we began to share our stories, it became abundantly clear that God had been preparing us all along for a time such as this. Everything we'd learned through the process of different jobs, various business ventures, diverse church experiences, and challenging life experiences was about to culminate into a beautiful ministry, where we were truly living out our dreams.

Nothing is for nothing, sweet sister; every tear, every heartache, every lost friendship, every failed marriage, every person you meet, and every job you hold is a stepping-stone to God's plan for your life.

> And we know that in all things God works for the good of those who love him, who have been called according to his purpose. (Romans 8:28 NIV)

Share a life circumstance that you thought at the time there was absolutely no way anything good could possibly come from this, but on the other side, you now see exactly why the Lord allowed you to walk through such a season:

_____

_____

_____

_____

_____

_____

Coming out on the other side of these life experiences is the big, beautiful life that God wants so badly for us as his daughters. Allow yourself to be open to the dreams the Lord has placed in you; commit to finding time to be in communion and prayer with him each day. Allow your mind to be freed from the clutter so that the Lord can truly speak to you.

God has an amazing plan for your life, but you have to be willing to say, "Not my will, Lord, but yours." This is where we begin to walk in freedom, step into our calling, and live out our truly happy and beautiful life. He wants it so badly for you, sweet sister; may we never forget that each one of us is his highest priority. He's still willing to leave the ninety-nine for you; he longs to wrap you in his love so you can dance deliriously happy in his glory and grace.

Closing Thoughts

In this journey called life, it's a fact that we will have hard times, seasons of struggle and disappointment. However, we can take heart that God, our precious heavenly Father, who created us in *his* image, does not leave us alone to face any situation. No way.

Rest assured, sweet sister, that he is walking right beside you through every struggle, every heartache, every trial, and every season.

> So be strong and courageous! Do not be afraid and do not panic before them. For the LORD your God will personally go ahead of you. He will neither fail you nor abandon you. (Deuteronomy 31:6 NLT)

Because of his amazing sacrifice through his son, Jesus Christ, we can live in complete freedom that we *are* who God says we are, not what the world tells us we are, not who the enemy tries to convince us we are, and not how we see ourselves. We are so, so much more in our Father's eyes.

Remember the list you shared early in the study about how you feel God sees you? Has it changed? Do you feel differently today than when you began walking this journey to the something beautiful God has in store for you? Share below how you feel God sees you today:

_____

_____

_____

_____

_____

_____

_____

This, ladies, is how God truly sees you…

A Daughter	Cute	Gorgeous	Radiant
Accepted	Dazzling	Graceful	Ravishing
Admirable	Delightful	Grand	Redeemed
Appealing	Divine	His	Righteous
Attractive	Elegant	Holy	Royalty
Beautiful	Empowered	Joyous	Saved
Beloved	Excellent	Lovely	Secure
Blessed	Exquisite	Magnificent	Stunning
Called	Fair	Marvelous	Treasured
Capable	Fascinating	Phenomenal	Unique
Charming	Forgiven	Powerful	Valuable
Chosen	Free	Precious	Wonderful
Classy	Gifted	Pure	Worthy

The list above contains fifty-two words to describe how our heavenly Father sees us. We could never begin to encompass all the words the Lord has to describe us as his daughters; however, these are a few we jotted down that we learned to claim over ourselves through the years. Our challenge to you as we conclude the study is that you take this list and, over the coming year, remind yourself how immeasurably loved you truly are by the Lord. Why not begin today? Start with the first word on the list; meditate on it throughout the coming week, and claim a new word for each week throughout the year ahead. As you wake up each morning, audibly remind yourself how God really sees you. And don't stop there; write it on your bathroom mirror, place a sticky note on the dash of your car, set a daily reminder on your cell phone or any other place where you will see it, and be reminded daily to speak God's truth to your heart. Read this sentence aloud: "My name is _____, and God says I am beautiful." Walk boldly, precious friend, in the confidence that you are what God says you are. You are his. Now go enjoy the beautiful life he has planned for you; it's yours, girl. All you have to do is walk it out. Your something beautiful is just now.

About the Authors

Hello, friends. My name is Amber Edwards, and I am absolutely thrilled you are here. Just so you'll have a little insight into who I am, you must know that my most important roles are that of wife to my wonderful husband, Michael, and mother to my two young adult children, Shelby and Zac. My family is everything to me. They challenge me each and every day to be the very best version of me I can be; simply put, they make me better. I have no idea what I ever did to deserve these three amazing souls in my life, but mere words cannot express how beyond blessed I feel the Lord chose me to pour into and do life alongside each of them. God is good.

I am a legal assistant/paralegal by trade, but my true passion is people. One of my spiritual gifts is encouragement; there's nothing that brings me more joy than doing something that makes someone smile. I rarely meet anyone who remains a stranger; I can, and will, talk to anyone. I have a wonderful tribe of friends, and although it's difficult with the busyness of life, I am very intentional about staying connected and making sure they know how much I value each of their roles in my story.

The older I get, the more I find it's the simplest things in life that put a smile on my face and immediately send me to my happy place, things like having my family together at church for worship, *all* things Christmas (yes, I'm a little over the top with it), a big ol' glass of iced tea, brunch with girlfriends, date night with my man, a walk on the beach at sunset, fresh flowers, Italian food, chocolate chip cookies, writing/journaling, just to name a few (and not necessarily in that order).

I was saved at a young age, and although I've gone through seasons of separation, I've always felt the Lord's hand and presence in my life. He has used every season, trial, and accomplishment to reveal my purpose and passions and make me the woman I am today.

My family and I attend Church of the Highlands in Birmingham, Alabama, where I am privileged to serve on the Dream Team as both an Events Team Leader and a Small Groups Coach for the Women's Team. The Lord has placed a passion for women deep inside my heart, and I am honored he has orchestrated a platform for me to minister in this area through both the written word and in growing a ministry. He's been telling me for a long time he has more for me, so I'm buckling up for the ride because I know it's going to be so much fun.

†††

Welcome to my happy place. I'm Jackie Tinkler, and I am a creative leader and organized eclectic who loves to write about God's Word and everyday things, uncovering something beautiful for each day. My favorite thing is drinking coffee, so if I were to meet you face to face, I would suggest we meet at a cozy café where we could get to know one another over a latte.

As a child, I lived in Upstate New York, where all of my family members lived within blocks and ate dinner together every Sunday. One day, the ocean called, and we left our city blocks to move to the beautiful beaches of Brevard County, Florida, where I started my family and was called to women's ministry. Many years later, the unexpected happened in the form of a job loss. God navigated it brilliantly, which made it okay. That experience opened an amazing door for my husband, Jim, and I to live a new adventure as empty-nesters in the Magic City of Birmingham, Alabama. I've always felt God had more for me. Setbacks may have put me behind a few years, but through my relationship with Jesus, I was able to overcome all of it. God opened doors of opportunity for me I never dreamed of. When life said, "It's over for you," God said, "I have more."

I've had the honor of being in women's ministry for over twenty years as a ministry director, biblical counselor, conference producer, and writer. My most cherished life's role has been growing in love with my husband, Jim, our adult daughter, Lauren, and our pillow-loving chocolate lab, Nelson. We attend Church of the Highlands in Birmingham, Alabama, where I have had the privilege of serving and doing life with amazing people. When I'm not writing, I can be found decorating cozy spaces, relaxing at a B&B, cooking a gourmet meal, or enjoying a great classic movie.